ENGLAND IN COLOUR

ENGLAND
in colour

ILLUSTRATED BY 60 COLOUR PHOTOGRAPHS

With an Introduction and
Commentaries by
JOHN BURKE

B. T. BATSFORD LTD LONDON

First published 1972

ISBN 0 7134 0026
Printed in the Netherlands
by De Lange/Van Leer
for the publishers
B. T. Batsford Ltd
4 Fitzhardinge Street, London, W.1

CONTENTS

ACKNOWLEDGMENTS

The Publishers wish to thank the following for the photographs appearing in this book:

Noel Habgood FRPS for pages 33, 45, 47, 49, 53, 61, 67, 81, 85, 87, 91, 94–95, 97, 103, 105, 113, 119, 131, 134–135, 139, 145, 153, 157, 159; A. F. Kersting AIIP, FRPS for pages 35, 37, 39, 43, 51, 55, 73, 89, 99, 101, 107, 109, 117, 127, 137, 141, 148–149; Kenneth Scowen FIIP, FRPS for pages 41, 57, 63, 65, 69, 71, 76–77, 79, 83, 111, 115, 121, 123, 125, 129, 143, 151, 155.

Introduction

What a pity it is that we have no amusements in England but vice and religion!

Sydney Smith

LISTENING TO THE jeremiads booming around our heads, we might suppose that in England today there is too little religion and far too much vice. The decline and collapse of all our virtues is foretold. England isn't what it was; but then, like *Punch*, it never was. The puritanical would have expressed the same distaste at any stage of our history. The bawdiness of Elizabeth I's time is now conceded to have been rather jolly and healthy – provided it is not quoted out loud in mixed company. The sniggering obscenities of the Restoration are allowed on the London stage because the plays have somehow become classics, and classics are different; and besides, the costumes are so gorgeous.

In the fury of the Great Fire of London the fanatical Solomon Eagle preached that it came as a punishment for the sins of the people. Prophets of doom have deplored, despaired and denounced throughout uncountable reigns. Painters, poets, architects and lovers of town and countryside have also despaired and denounced. In each generation there are those who wish to sweep away the mess their ancestors have made, and those who wish to preserve the glories their ancestors have created; those who long to march more briskly into a promising future, and those who want to resist all change until the last possible minute.

England for our children and grandchildren – what will it be, and how much of it will they feel grateful for? How much, indeed, is there still left for the enrichment of our own generation?

The pictures in this book attempt to capture certain scenes and moods before they are distorted or even swept away altogether. Of course the task is a nearly impossible one. Within seconds of a photograph having been taken, the scene is already changing. No picture of England can be anything but transient. England does not exist in the present: it is only a line, too thin to measure, between an advancing tomorrow and a receding yesterday. It's hard to distinguish clear outlines ahead. Things in the past do look so much more settled and substantial. Yet to those who had to live through those yesterdays and play their part in shaping them, the times were just as confused and confusing as our own. There was never a stage at which anyone was powerful enough to be a cosmic Canute and say: 'That's enough – leave well alone, nothing must be altered from now on.'

A street corner on the outskirts of Bury St Edmunds is partially obstructed by an old hummock of stone. A girl on her way to school from a suburban side street may pass it a dozen times a week and will know it as the Plague Stone. One day, instead of taking it for granted, she may start to ask questions. What plague? And what part did the stone play?

In fact the hollow in the top was filled with vinegar so that farmers bringing food from the countryside to the edge of the plague-stricken town could take payment from coins dropped into this antiseptic pool. But once started on the story, we find it goes further back. The stone was not hollowed out specifically for the vinegar: it was once the base and socket for a wooden cross marking the limit of the Abbey's jurisdiction. The Abbey? That same one at whose great altar the barons swore mutual loyalty until they could force Magna Carta from King John.

A Liverpool boy sauntering towards the Pier Head to watch the modern traffic of a great port may cross the Goree without querying the origin of the name or wondering about the traffic which once made it prosperous. It was the assembly point for slaves whose sale and shipment formed the basis of so much of Liverpool's wealth.

Once you start delving – into words, into history, into the soil itself – there is no end to it.

A ploughshare strikes a fragment of buried metal, and an ancient treasure is unearthed. Maiden Castle in Dorset disgorges tools and pottery testifying to an occupation lasting from 2000 B.C. to Roman times. A lonely, windswept barrow proves to be the richly furnished tomb of some lost, pagan chieftain. And everywhere are legends and supposed relics of one inspiringly regal figure who may be only the symbolic fusion of many minor tribal leaders – but one in which we romantically love to believe. According to the chronicler Geoffrey of Monmouth he was grandson of the Emperor Constantine, at first a defender of Roman traditions against the heathen Saxons and then a warrior against Rome itself. In Wales the poems speak of him as an emperor and describe his quest for a magic cauldron. Later stories tell of a quest for the Holy Grail, and the remote, half-mystical figure becomes that of King Arthur.

His father, Uther Pendragon, was said to have lived in a castle at Tintagel long before the present one was built. On the beach below is what is known as Merlin's Cave. A sunken causeway running through the marshy land between Cadbury and Glastonbury is mentioned in many Arthurian chronicles. From Cadbury he is recorded as having set out to find his sword Excalibur. Glastonbury has been associated with the Isle of Avalon where he was buried. Shortly after the death of Henry II it was reported that the monks had found a coffin containing the bones of King Arthur and Queen Guinevere and had placed them in a casket among the abbey's treasures. But then, in 1278 a tomb opened there in the presence of Edward I and Queen Eleanor was recorded as holding the bones of Arthur and Guinevere, which were wrapped in silk and once more interred. The tomb was destroyed at the Reformation, but its base was rediscovered in 1931.

Hic jacet Arthurus, rex quondam, rex futurus.

The once and future king. . . . Every nation has its mythical saviour who will one day emerge from a long slumber and take his rightful place at the head of his people. A statue known to every Danish schoolchild shows Holger Danske drowsing over his shield, waiting for the call. Under Blanik Hill in Czechoslovakia lies a troop of Bohemian knights which will one crucial day be led out by St Wenceslas. Arthur sleeps in Avalon until the hour of England's greatest need. There have been times when even the most devout believers in his existence could be forgiven for wondering if he had overslept.

Arthur's associations with various parts of the land may be apocryphal, but there have been other, more solid kings and queens who come vividly to life again as one moves from place to place. Names and dates, dull and uninspiring in school, take on meaning in their proper setting. Here an echo of King Alfred; the emblem of Henry VIII in chiselled stone; a ruin that Cromwell knocked about a bit.

We don't learn England all of a piece. What is this island, anyway, and who are the English? They are Celts, Britons, Angles, Saxons, Danes, Normans – Jews, Catholics, Anglicans and Nonconformists. In Cornwall the people are still more akin to the Bretons than to their supposed fellow countrymen in, say, Lancashire. The Northumbrian voice sounds more like Jutland Danish than Oxford English. Dutch blood was often shed off the coasts of East Anglia, but there is also much of it running vigorously in Lincolnshire, Norfolk and Suffolk veins. If we are a nation of shopkeepers, as Napoleon thought, how explain our seamen, our miners and mountaineers? Admirals, poets, endearing wastrels and not so endearing wastrels; reformers and those in need of reform – some conditioned by the smugness of their upbringing, others by its starkness. Some meditative among dreaming spires, others weatherbeaten, dominated by or exhilarated by the raging seas. The incredible variety of their settings and achievements is there to be seen in the following pages.

The joy of piecing together the jigsaw is not merely in a gradual understanding of one's own town or valley, rewarding though that must be. There are also the enticing, provocative places in between, glimpsed from road or railway and related to one another at first haphazardly, then with a developing sense of the pattern. One day, you say, I'll stop there instead of just rushing through: I'll have a better look, I've heard about it, I'm sure there's more to see and hear.

Edward Thomas, in a train stopping briefly at a small station on a hot June afternoon, was captured just by a name and an atmosphere:

The steam hissed. Someone cleared his throat.
No one left and no one came
On the bare platform. What I saw
Was Adlestrop – only the name.

Only the name. But names are so evocative. Names with old meanings half forgotten, names twisted and forced into new syllables, taken from Old Norse and Old English and Norman French and Latin, and given an English nudge: they lead into fascinating by-ways and to strange places. St Thomas the Apostle becomes in due course 'Stinkbottle', and the fact that the town rubbish tip is placed on that tract of ground in this century leads even local inhabitants to suppose that the name is a contemporary jibe rather than the corruption of an ancient dedication.

I can still recite the sequence of little halts along a Sussex railway line I knew when I was a child, and at once the past is recaptured – sight, sound, smell and feel of it.

I was born in Rye, and during my lifetime the houses in Church Square have looked pretty much as they do in our picture. Sentimental as most people are about their own background, I wish everything to be as it always was. Yet I loved to read science-fiction, thought it essential that man should get to the Moon, and only a few yards from those Church Square houses was entranced one evening by something which my parents and grandparents regarded as destructive of all they most approved. Through an open window I heard a broadcast direct from America – an incredible thing in those days – of Count Basie's orchestra. Kansas City jazz in a Tudor and Georgian cobbled street? It was absurd; but I adored it. If I am irritated today by a 16-year-old swinging a transistor radio along the pavement below my window, what right do I, of all people, really have to pontificate? At what stage does one peevishly set into the mood of 'Thus far and no farther'?

Before the Second World War there was a tramway carrying holidaymakers and golfers from Rye to the golf links and to Camber Sands. I knew every inch of the way, every note struck by the wheels from the lines as they ran over grass and gravel, over a resounding bridge above a marsh dyke, and then over the shingle. A haunting resonance was set up for a moment as the engine and coaches passed the golf links station and the harbour-master's house. Even today I can sense – though all too remotely and irreclaimably – the anticipation as we jogged round that slow curve and approached the wooden shack of Camber Sands station. Sometimes the tide came in so far that shallow water lay gleaming immediately below the embankment. The low beach-banks were bright, the water dazzled, the sky was immense. Always (surely memory cannot be at fault on this point) the sun shone. Writing an article about the tram some 20 years ago, I see that I concluded: 'In a few years, I realise with shame, I shall almost certainly be saying, "We don't have summers like we did when I was a boy."' And I have this moment only just prevented myself from doing just that.

We carried a bag crammed with bathing costumes, beach shoes, sandwiches, thermos flask and a bottle of fizzy lemonade. There were magazines bought perhaps on Hastings Pier the previous day, when one received a free copy of an old *Happy Magazine* with a twopenny copy of *Answers* or *Titbits.*

The hard-running, wooden-seated coaches were drawn either by an old steam locomotive or by a little petrol engine. The steam engine would be more highly regarded nowadays, but at the time the petrol tram was much more individualistic than a mere steam engine, of which there were plenty pulling ordinary, everyday trains.

The army used the line during the war. Once when I came to Rye under the intermittent snarl of V-1 weapons, I saw the engine standing out in the rain, the sheds falling to pieces, the coaches neglected. After the war, I thought, they'll have a job putting this to rights.

After the war. . . . The tramway is gone, considered not worthy of renovation. Doubtless there were good financial reasons. There usually are.

Today there is a large holiday camp at Camber. It would be churlish to begrudge thousands of holidaymakers the pleasures which only a few hundred of us knew then; but it is a pity that, in buses or their own cars, they will never savour that particular delight, the bumpy journey along the resounding track towards the quiet expanses of marram grass, sand dunes and shore, and the return journey into the sunset. When, years later, I lived for a time in Rye, I often looked out across the levels and, when the wind was in the right direction, could fancy that I heard the familiar puttering noise as the tram came along the last straight into the terminus.

For me, and I hope for everybody, there are other memories in this book. It is a long time since I was in Northumberland, but the mere thought of it makes me impatient to be there again. Oxford during the war, Cambridge afterwards: as a strolling outsider I have always had a strong preference for Cambridge, which any good Oxford man could surely prove in a matter of minutes to be irrational, without making the slightest dent in my convictions.

Trafalgar Square, I observe, no longer has the kiosk we knew in the war years. Troops on leave could collect free tickets donated by London theatres, and there was always a queue before opening time to grab the limited number available for the Windmill Theatre. The girls of the Windmill were regarded as very daring then. If such a kiosk existed today, what would be the queue's priorities? For myself, I always seemed to arrive when the remaining tickets were for experimental plays in blank verse out at Hammersmith.

Salisbury and Stonehenge have personal memories, and also memories of my favourite writer of the English language. William Hazlitt stayed frequently at an inn called Winterslow Hut a couple of miles from Salisbury, where his chief happiness, according to his son's memoir, was *the thorough quiet of the place, the sole interruption of which was the passage, to and fro, of the London mails.* The road is now the A.30.

In his *Farewell to Essay-Writing*, written at Winterslow, Hazlitt mused:

> *We walk through life, as through a narrow path, with a thin curtain drawn around it; behind are ranged rich portraits, airy harps are strung – yet we will not stretch forth our hands and lift aside the veil. . . . We have only at any time to 'peep through the*

blanket of the past', to possess ourselves at once of all that has regaled our senses, that is stored up in our memory, that has struck our fancy, that has pierced our hearts: – yet to all this we are indifferent, insensible, and seem intent only on the present vexation, the future disappointment.

Other pictures, other visions. I remember a day in Lavenham Market Place with a painter friend who was professionally curious about the skill of a lady seated on a stool in the middle of the square, facing the magnificent Guildhall and painting earnestly away at her easel. We crept round in the usual pseudo-diffident way and gave the canvas a quick glance in passing. The good lady was painting a roseate picture of a vase of flowers. We were baffled, and have remained so to this day. Perhaps at the very moment of my writing these words that same lady is sitting at home before a vase of flowers, assiduously painting a picture of Lavenham Guildhall.

And what should they know of England who only England know?

Visitors from abroad often see us more clearly than we can hope to see ourselves. And if we, for our own part, go abroad on holiday or on business or in the armed forces, what shift of perspective is there for *us* when we return? Some come home with their detestation of foreigners and all things foreign comfortably confirmed. Others find that proportions have subtly altered. Seen after a spell in Italy or Scandinavia or the United States our homeland can be, just for a little while before we are rehabilitated, a tantalisingly foreign country. How good for the appetite if we could retain from now on some trace of that alien flavour!

Coventry Cathedral was brutally destroyed by young savages in the grip of an old evil. Bombs ripped the flesh and fabric of London. It was hideous: what was done can never be undone; neither love nor technical ingenuity can replace what has gone; yet there could have been much more, much worse. Supposing England had been occupied as France, Belgium and Holland were occupied? Suppose, when the longed-for liberation came, that our deliverers tested range and elevation of their guns, as the Allies did in France, on church steeples? Think of Blythburgh gone, of New Romney as a coldly calculated artillery target, of Alfriston and Chilham, Louth and Earls Barton.

And then think of our own countrymen who today, with no military excuse and no need to call on the heavy artillery, are methodically destroying our towns and villages for, no doubt, the best of motives.

What will a picture-book of 2072 show, if there are such outmoded things as books by 2072?

London grows uncontrollably and yet is disappearing. After the war it was vowed that there would never again be the random building which had disfigured it from the end of the nineteenth century onwards. St Paul's, exposed on all sides by bombing and at last showing its full beauty, would never again be hemmed in. Idealistic planners and enlightened administrators would ensure that the new London combined all that was best of the old and the new.

The fulfilment of these promises is to be seen in Shell Centre, Centre Point, the Barbican, the squared-up skyscraper which ensures that the silhouette of Southwark Cathedral is banished from the skyline, and the indescribable monster thrusting out of Ludgate Hill to obstruct the view of St Paul's.

There are Englishmen who fight to preserve what is best from the past. The National Trust watches over as much of the countryside as it can encompass, and is the public's custodian of many great houses and gardens which would otherwise have been perverted long ago to the uses of some greedy entrepreneur or even greedier Government department. The Conservation Corps of hard-working young volunteers – rather more young people, though less publicised, than are to be found exposing themselves to supposed corruption in basement clubs and pornographic cinemas – fight a dogged battle against the destruction of hedges, footpaths, wildlife reserves, the disappearance of canals and copses, the encroachment of industrial waste on our already poisoned farmland, and the callous upsetting of the whole ecological balance of our fields and hills.

Perhaps succeeding generations will feel no regret for the losses we already regret. What our children have not known, they cannot miss. Their England will not be ours, and this is not to say that it will be worse. But they may come to experience their own nostalgia. I foresee a preservationist outcry against proposals to demolish that much-loved old twentieth-century landmark, the Post Office Tower (seen in this book peeping like an extra-terrestrial invader over the shrubbery in Queen Mary's Garden) in order to make way for . . . well, for what? As I have said earlier, we cannot descry the outlines of the future. Will the blocks of flats on Putney Hill be scheduled under preservation orders; will Leicester University be the tourist trap of the twenty-first century; will the National Trust charge an entrance fee for the upkeep of the picturesque multi-storey car park in Hertford, and the Fylingdales Early Warning Station globes be bought at scrap prices for an industrial museum?

Flavours and emotions are blunted as the years go by. Perhaps there will never again be the tangy immediacy of the love and laughter in Tynemouth and (of all improbable but happily remembered places) Newcastle, or the first ecstatic shock on seeing Durham Cathedral, or the insidious and forever hypnotic smell of woodsmoke along the river Tillingham. Perhaps all the mature satisfactions to be derived from listening to the music of Englishmen such as Purcell, Byrd and Dowland cannot quite match the exaltation from hearing Count Basie in that cobbled street.

Not all tastes grow too bland, not all perceptions are necessarily blurred by the passage of time. Some things are best apprehended in a flash of revelation, others come more slowly into focus. I see more of my country and see it more clearly than I could have done 30 or 40 years ago. The visitor from abroad will not have the time for this process to work, but as hosts we can hope that his intermittent mental snapshots will, when taken home and sorted out into some kind of order, provide an enriching private landscape.

'I hate England', the angry playwright John Osborne was reported as saying a few years ago. Down on his head came the predictable storm of patriotic abuse. Yet I would hazard a guess, strengthened by what he reveals in his more recent plays, that Osborne's hatred was only the dark side of his love, and equally justified. Like many of us, he was enraged by the failings and blemishes which made his England less lovable than the true patriot, as opposed to the noisy chauvinist, would wish it to be.

There is room for hate. Too many green fields are buried beneath a different green, sour with slag heaps. Too many motorways and airstrips have gashed the living earth. The magnificent Durham coast is a black horror from the wastefulness and negligence of coal profiteers and their no less wanton successors. The Potteries glow vigorously in Arnold Bennett's novels but shed a harsher, more shrivelling glow on those who have to live there. Yet those of us who drive from one beauty spot to another, or spend a leisurely holiday in some attractive old fishing port, would be unable to afford such luxuries without the factories and mines and their destructive breath.

And even the industrial landscape can sometimes tempt the wanderer away from more picturesque lanes and hilltops. Telford's great aqueducts and viaducts are as much an imposition on nature as the towering electricity pylons of our own day, but have bedded themselves nobly into the land. Drainage windmills may have been a prettier sight on the Fens than later pumping-houses, but the great wheel and gleaming mechanism of Stretham Old Engine above its now drowsy waterway have a grandeur of their own, even if not of the same order as that of nearby Ely Cathedral. The derelict villages and crumbling gear of Cornish mines have an eerie allure at twilight; and what better use for an abandoned quarry at Crich in Derbyshire than as a museum for all shapes, sizes and colours of old trams?

The itinerary sketched out in the following pages takes us on a journey from the south-east of England up through London and on to the north-east, then over the spine of the country and down at last to the extreme western tip of the mainland. The late John Gloag observed that England is a living guidebook to over two thousand years of civilisation. The same can obviously be said, with just as much fervour, of Italy and France. But we like to feel we have distinctive features to offer, a certain special atmosphere, something inimitable in our snug, even smug, little villages, in the snowy ridges and combes, the great palaces and remote farms, the placid or turbulent river valleys, and the ruins faintly reverberating with old romance or old violence.

The knowledgeable traveller has every right to protest that

a hundred exquisite scenes have been neglected. Nothing from Shropshire, not a glimpse of Huntingdon or the Essex creeks? No Alnwick Castle, no dreaming Chelsworth, none of Winchester's splendours? Such protest is in itself praise. However much we may righteously grumble about despoliation, there is still so much left to see. For my own part, I have been fortunate in my lifetime so far in discovering so much, and more fortunate in knowing that even now I have only to turn off a road almost boring in its familiarity to find yet one more corner that is utterly new though it may have been there for centuries. The jolt of an unexpected ugliness is softened by the balm of a neighbouring beauty.

Some of the things we seek to preserve are, to be honest, grotesque. It is natural that we should cling to what we have loved, but surely not that England should become a storeroom of soiled, shattered toys of no intrinsic value which we haven't the heart or the good taste to throw away. There are cherished ancient monuments which are eyesores. There are new buildings which scare us with their newness but are beautiful.

The future is difficult. But then, it always was.

John Constable's name appears more than once in this book for the good reason that he was a great Englishman who did and said fine things. Let him have the last word:

Fashion always had, and will have, its day;
but truth in all things only will last, and
can only have just claims on posterity.

John Burke

The Plates

Beachy Head, Sussex

Below the 570-ft chalk cliff, the highest on the south coast, the lighthouse at night transmits a beam visible 16 miles out in the English Channel. Like the other lighthouses and lightships of the seas about this island, it comes under the jurisdiction of the Corporation of Trinity House, funds being provided from special Light Dues levied on shipping using United Kingdom ports.

Westward are the Seven Sisters, a rolling switchback of cliffs whose shallows are the remnants of ancient river valleys which descended into the sea before erosion chopped the land away to its present shape.

The name of Beachy Head has nothing to do with beaches but is a corruption of the Norman French *Le Beau Chef.* A celebrated Norman duke landed a few miles to the east on the shores of Pevensey Bay in 1066 and marched unchecked to Hastings, where he defeated the Saxon Harold and went down in history and on local inn signs as William the Conqueror.

In 1690 the French defeated combined Dutch and English fleets off the headland.

This same stretch of coast was included in Adolf Hitler's 1940 plan for an invasion after the Royal Air Force had been 'so reduced morally and physically' that it would be powerless to offer any significant resistance, while a large part of the Royal Navy was to be tied down and its home-based forces crippled by air and torpedo attack. The equation was, for one reason and another, not resolved in accordance with these calculations.

The South Downs near Telscombe, Sussex

Two ridges of whalebacked hills face each other across the Weald. The North Downs run on into Kent, the South Downs reach the sea at Beachy Head. Rudyard Kipling wrote adoringly of them; Hilaire Belloc remembered them when in the 'sodden and unkind' Midlands, and declared that of all memories these would be sharpest

> *whenever by some evil fortune a Sussex man dies*
> *far away from home.*

Telscombe is one of the few hamlets on the Downs above the 200-ft level, but in the distant past were many settlements whose traces can still be identified. The first sheep brought from Spain by the Carthaginians or from Gaul by Celts and Romans would have browsed over the thousands of acres which retain traces of early farming. Here was developed the mighty Southdown breed. While eighteenth-century flocks grazed, their shepherds passed the time catching wheatears to augment their meagre diet and meagre income. One such, John Dudeney, recorded:

> *I had a good mother and father, though they were*
> *poor, my father's wages being only £30 a year,*
> *and the keeping of ten or twelve sheep, having a*
> *family of ten children, yet we were never in want.*

The loneliness suited Dudeney. He dug a hole on the hillside, covered it with a large flint, and kept books there and a slate on which he worked at geometry. Eventually he left the shepherd's life to become a schoolmaster in the county town, Lewes.

The Royal Pavilion, Brighton, Sussex

The fishing village known originally as Brighthelmstone was developing into a holiday centre as early as 1736, when a visitor wrote to a friend in London:

> *My morning's business is bathing in the sea; and then buying fish; and my evening occupation is riding out for air, viewing the old Saxon camps, and counting the ships in the road and the boats that are trawling . . . . the coast is safe, and the cannons all covered with rust and grass, the ships moored, no enemy apprehended.*

This contradicts a long-held belief that it was Dr Richard Russell of Lewes who 'invented' sea bathing here in 1750; but there is little doubt that Russell's enthusiastic medical recommendations really established Brighton as a fashionable resort.

The Prince of Wales paid his first visit in 1782 and built the Royal Pavilion so that he might have a seaside home for several months of the year. Henry Holland's basic design was classical, with a pastiche Chinese interior, but John Nash was later engaged to transform it with exuberant pinnacles and minarets. At a time of national poverty, the Prince's extravagance as Regent and later as George IV provoked bitter resentment: he lavished fortunes on meals for his guests, sometimes offering a choice from 100 dishes at a time, created by the celebrated Carême.

Today the Pavilion has fine displays of glass and furniture. The Dome, of which Sydney Smith commented that it looked as if the dome of St Paul's had come here and pupped, has become a conference and concert hall.

Bodiam Castle, Sussex

Rising from a lake creamy with water lilies, this is everyone's idea of a romantic stronghold from which spotless knights galloped out to rescue fair maidens from dragons and other afflictions. Unfortunately its history is relatively uneventful.

Building was begun in 1386 by Sir Edward Dalyngruge. In the company of the notorious Edward Knollys and other bandits, Sir Edward had spent a profitable time roaming the French countryside killing, robbing, and holding widows or single women of property to ransom. He returned with enough spoils to erect a castle on a site which came to him when he married the heiress to the land; and, as the French were carrying out some vengeful raids of their own, he had good reason to surround himself with strong fortifications at this strategic point in the Rother valley, in those days an estuary. The French, however, though attacking Rye, Winchelsea and Hastings, never reached Bodiam.

The castle is 160-ft square, and its thick circular towers are 70-ft high. Neglected for centuries, it was in danger of defeat not from enemy assault but from the inroads of ivy and decay, which reduced it to no more than a picturesque shell. Finally restored and presented to the nation by Lord Curzon of Kedleston, it is now under the care of the National Trust.

Church Square, Rye, Sussex

The inscription above the parish church clock declares that 'our time is a very shadow that passeth away', but in spite of the intrusion of a holiday camp, a caravan site, a rash of olde-worlde tea-shoppes and the interminable flow of traffic during the summer months, time has somehow been restrained from fleeing too swiftly through Rye. Its cobbled streets have not yet relinquished their grip on a proud past.

Rye stood for centuries on the sea, with shipbuilding as a major industry. It partnered Winchelsea as one of the two Ancient Towns granted full partnership in the Cinque Ports, whose responsibility it was from the twelfth century onwards to fight the King's enemies in the Channel, police the home seas against pirates, and convey troops to any areas where the King might wish to give battle. The sea began to recede in the sixteenth century and is now two miles away, but fishing boats still come up the Rother to the quays.

Ypres Tower recalls a Norman Earl of Kent, and served as the last refuge for townsfolk during French raids. A Flemish word on a Church Square letter-box reminds us of those who fled here, as so many have done throughout the centuries, from religious persecution.

John Fletcher, Elizabethan dramatist, was born here. Henry James lived in Lamb House and wrote much of his later work in its garden room, destroyed by Second World War bombing. Painters, potters and writers work here today. Rye is still a living entity, not merely a show-place.

Canterbury Cathedral, Kent

Canterbury was an important centre long before Roman times, and in due course became the capital of the pagan kings of Kent. Christianity was brought in 597 by St Augustine, who founded a Benedictine priory, burnt in 1011 by the Danes. Lanfranc, the first Norman archbishop, undertook the creation of a new cathedral, a work continued by his successors and consecrated in 1130.

On a December day in 1170 four knights, goaded by Henry II's demand as to why nobody would rid him of his troublesome priest, stormed in at vespers and murdered Thomas à Becket, whose shrine thereafter became one of the most important destinations for pilgrims from all over Europe. Geoffrey Chaucer's *The Canterbury Tales* relates in heroic couplets the story of a group of pilgrims preparing to set out for the shrine from a London inn. They enliven the journey by telling stories on the way out and the way back, as many similar groups must have done. The existing nave was erected in Chaucer's own day out of the cathedral's profits from such pilgrimages.

The rebuilt priory nearby was again ravaged when Cromwell's men set upon it. The gatehouse remains, leading now to a college established in the last century for the training of Anglican missionaries. The Puritans also destroyed much stained glass in the cathedral, but what remains is among the finest in the land.

Of the two west towers shown in the picture, the nearer was erected between 1440 and 1452, the northern one in 1832 after an earlier tower had been demolished to make way for one which would match its neighbour.

The River Thames at Pangbourne, Berkshire

In the year before his death, Edward the Confessor commanded of the administrators of the royal rivers:

> *If mills, fisheries or other works are constructed to their hindrance, let these works be destroyed, the waters repaired, and the forfeit to the King not forgotten.*

The greed of later generations has flouted the royal decree, the clear waters have been fouled, and the pageantry of the Thames at London has given way to the noise and effluent of commerce; but here and there along the 200 miles from its twin sources in the Cotswolds are still to be found tranquil, unpolluted reaches.

Six miles above Reading the bourne of the Pang enters the Thames. On a hill above is the Nautical College founded in 1917. Kenneth Grahame, for whose son *The Wind in the Willows* was written, found peace here after that son's tragic death, died and was buried here; but later his body was moved to his beloved Oxford and interred in Holywell cemetery. At the whispering water's edge one thinks inevitably of Mole, Rat, and the ebullient Mr Toad.

The River Thames at Windsor, Berkshire

The river skirts the castle and Home Park on three sides, the winding course between its shores giving the name of Windesore to the town.

Edward the Confessor had made a gift of his Old Windsor palace to Westminster Abbey. A few years after the Battle of Hastings, William the Conqueror took it for his own and set about constructing a moated castle which, through various transformations, has been a royal residence ever since.

Henry I kept court here, Henry II held a great council in 1175. King John stayed here in no very good humour when due to meet the barons at Runnymede to set his seal on Magna Carta. Henry III finished the walls and set up three towers. Edward III pulled a lot of it down and refashioned it according to his own concepts. Edward IV began St George's Chapel; Henry VII completed the nave; for the roof over the choir we are indebted to Henry VIII. Here they lived, and here are the tombs of many of them.

The body of Charles I, terrible witness to Cromwell's promise that 'We will cut off the King's head with the crown on it', was brought here on a snowy February morning in 1649 to be buried in a lead wrapping without any religious service, since the sonorous phrases of the Prayer-Book had by now been proscribed.

Queen Victoria and her Consort, Prince Albert, lie outside the castle walls, in a mausoleum in the Home Park.

Windsor Castle, Berkshire

The dominant feature of the fortress is the huge shell keep, with a few diminutive buildings inside, known as the Round Tower, though strictly speaking it is by no means round. Set by Edward III on a mound established by the Conqueror, it stands between the castle proper and the area containing St George's Chapel with its deanery and cloisters, known as the Lower Ward. Originally the mound was surrounded by its own ditch, of which a few traces remain to the south.

The view from the top of the tower commands 15 counties. Close at hand is Eton, and cutting through the richly wooded park one can see the Long Walk, once famous for its row of elm trees, felled in 1945 and replaced by plane and chestnut.

Henry VIII built the castle gateway which, with its royal coat of arms, is now the main public entrance, though there is also a way to the lower terrace up what are known as the Hundred Steps from Thames Street. He was also responsible for the north terrace, a favourite haunt of his daughter Elizabeth I. At one end of it Chaucer is believed to have stayed during the time he was in charge of building operations. From this terrace one can visit the enchanting microcosm of the Queen's Doll's House, presented by the public to Queen Mary in 1924.

NOTICE

Ascot, Berkshire

Ascot is a small yet spaciously proportioned town near the southern boundary of Windsor Great Park. Its nineteenth-century church has a brass memorial to Earl Roberts, the hero of Kandahar, whose last home was nearby and who was a regular member of the congregation before going to France at the outbreak of the First World War. Its main fame, however, derives not from memories of military gallantry but from its race meetings.

Queen Anne founded the racecourse in 1711, but it did not begin to reach its full potential until the Duke of Cumberland began to keep his stud at Cumberland Lodge in the Great Park.

England is a paradise for women, and a hell for horses.

So the melancholic Robert Burton. At Ascot both are pampered, and meet on equal terms. Or almost equal terms: perhaps during Royal Ascot week in June the hats have just a slight edge over the hoofs. During this fashionable event in what is still known as The Season, the Gold Cup and the Hunt Cup are supposedly the main draw; but the most impressive spectacle is undoubtedly the appearance of the Royal Family in open carriages drawn by the most aristocratic of horses and accompanied by resplendent footmen and outriders.

FOURTH

Hampton Court Palace, Middlesex

Officially designated a 'royal palace not in the personal occupation of the Sovereign', Hampton Court on the north bank of the Thames was begun as a private residence by Cardinal Wolsey in 1514. When he was brought down by his enemies, among them Anne Boleyn – whom he called 'the night crow' – Henry VIII took full possession and added many features, including the ornate vaulted roof of the Chapel Royal. The court on which Henry loved to play Royal Tennis still functions as the oldest tennis court left in Europe.

Of Wolsey's original vision, the first court remains but the brickwork of the west front has been substantially adapted and restored. Sir Christopher Wren was responsible for the east and south-east fronts and the court behind them, and also for the lion gates of the north entrance.

The orangery and gardens are justly famous. A baffling maze was constructed in William III's time, and a grapevine planted in 1769 still flourishes. Inside, the State rooms and others, which may be visited by the public, contain some notable paintings, tapestries and furniture.

Five of Henry VIII's wives lived here, and the ghost of Catherine Howard is said to haunt one of the galleries. Oliver Cromwell occupied the palace while Lord Protector, and his daughter was married in the Chapel Royal.

The complex of buildings contains over 50 'grace and favour residences' occupied by favour of the Sovereign.

CAR PARK

The Tower of London and Tower Bridge

The Tower began in the time of William the Conqueror with the erection of the keep, generally known as the White Tower because for some centuries from the thirteenth onwards its outer walls were whitewashed. Major additions were made by Richard Coeur de Lion, Henry III and Edward III, who added an outer curtain and the watergate of St Thomas's Tower. Henry VIII carried out further work around the perimeter. The present mock-medieval walls date only from mid-Victorian times.

The keepers of the fortress are known as Yeomen Warders and still sport a uniform dating from Henry VII's time. The commander bears the title of Constable of the Royal Palace and Fortress of London, and has a Lieutenant to aid him; but neither now lives on the premises.

Many a royal personage and many a fallen favourite of royalty has been incarcerated here; and many met their death on the block whose site is marked near the Chapel of St Peter ad Vincula. Captured rebels were often brought from Westminster by water and led to their doom through the wide arch of Traitors' Gate, opposite the Bloody Tower. Henry VIII married Catherine of Aragon, and disposed of a couple of other unwanted wives, within these walls.

Tower Bridge, opened in 1894, is 800-ft long between the landward towers and 200-ft between the towers rising from the river. The footway joining the tops of the towers was closed many years ago. Each of the two bascules, lifted hydraulically to allow shipping to pass beneath, weighs about 1,000 tons.

Buckingham Palace, London

Although representatives of foreign nations are still accredited to the Court of St James's, Buckingham Palace superseded St James's Palace as the London residence of the Sovereign after the accession of Queen Victoria.

It takes its name from the house built for the Duke of Buckingham in 1703 and bought for George III in 1762. It was later settled on Queen Charlotte, and passed to her son, Prince Regent and later George IV, who commissioned John Nash in 1824 to remodel it. The present Portland stone frontage dates from 1913. Edward VII, who referred to it during the more sombre years of his mother's widowhood as 'the sepulchre', was born and died in the palace, and the three sons of Elizabeth II were born here.

The Queen's Gallery, with a changing selection of pictures and works of art from the royal collections, is open to the public on certain days. The Royal Mews are also open on Wednesdays and Thursdays throughout the year – save in Ascot Week.

The forecourt is patrolled by sentries of the Brigade of Guards in full dress uniform. At 11.30 a.m. every day a band marches at the head of a new detachment on to the forecourt, and after the ceremony of Changing the Guard leads the off-duty guard back to barracks.

When the Sovereign is in residence, the Royal Standard flies at the masthead.

The Life Guards, London

While sentry duty at Buckingham Palace is carried out by one of the five regiments of the Foot Guards, another picket is mounted every morning at the Horse Guards by units of the Household Cavalry – the Life Guards, the Royal Horse Guards and the 1st Dragoons. The Life Guards are distinguished by white plumes on their helmets and red tunics, the Blues and Royals have red plumes and blue uniforms.

The barracks known as the Horse Guards was built over a segment of the old Whitehall Palace by William Kent in 1755 as a conversion for the headquarters of the General Staff, which they remained until 1872. Kent had to work according to rigid specifications laid down by Lord Burlington, and finished with a motley collection of ill-proportioned buildings. The clock tower looking out towards St James's Park is a sprightly feature of the landscape, but the arch of the drive-through is so low that Hogarth maliciously painted a cartoon of a coach emerging with a decapitated driver.

Today two mounted troopers on patient steeds occupy the sentry-boxes for hourly shifts between 10 a.m. and 4 p.m. daily. At 11 a.m. the formal ceremony of Changing the Guard takes place; 10 a.m. on Sundays.

On Horse Guards parade beyond, the Household Cavalry join the Brigade of Guards in the pageant of Trooping the Colour on the Sovereign's official birthday, usually celebrated on the second Saturday in June; and a mounted escort is provided at the State Opening of Parliament.

St James's Park, London

West of Horse Guards Parade and flanking the Mall between Buckingham Palace and Admiralty Arch, this green oasis with its ornamental lake and flower-fringed pathways was once a tract of marsh owned by a leper hospital standing where St James's Palace now stands. Henry VIII had the area drained and converted into a deer park. Charles II turned it into pleasure gardens. We owe its present layout to the indefatigable John Nash.

Paris had been nobly refashioned in accordance with the dictates of Napoleon. The Prince Regent wished his London to surpass it. Given his royal patron's support, Nash envisaged a pattern which would impose coherence on the whole tangled area between the Prince Regent's home in Carlton House and Marylebone Park, now to be renamed Regent's Park. A triumphal 'royal mile' predictably designated Regent Street was to provide a broad thoroughfare from this large park to the smaller expanse of St James's.

Many of Nash's schemes failed to materialise quite as he had seen them, and when they did they soon fell prey to the Philistines. In St James's Park, however, he succeeded in his aim. The dimensions are right, the skilfully angled paths may be crowded today but have not lost their charm; and the waterway which he reshaped into a gently curving lake has become a delightful preserve for the breeding of water-fowl.

Queen Mary's Garden, Regent's Park, London

At the northern extremity of John Nash's ambitious scheme for a more gracious London was the remnant of Middlesex Forest transformed into Marylebone Park. In 1818 it was, in our twentieth-century terms, scheduled for redevelopment, and Nash's plans for it would give, according to a diarist of the time,

> *a sort of glory to the Regent's government which will be more felt by remote posterity than the victories of Trafalgar and Waterloo.*

Two eminent societies established their headquarters here at an early stage. The Zoological Society of London, founded in 1824, applied two years later for the use of some 20 acres of the park but for a while had to be content with a mere five acres. The Royal Botanic Society, founded in 1838, received a royal charter the following year and permission to use a section of the park. Queen Victoria was its first patroness.

The Zoo remains. The Royal Botanic Society was dissolved in 1932, and the care of its gardens became the responsibility of the Royal Parks Department. Queen Mary, wife of George V, had always taken the deepest interest in its work and was greatly concerned about the future of the land for which it had been responsible. The garden, noted especially for its beautiful rosarium, bears her name as a token of the affection she showed for it.

Westminster Abbey, London

Within this Collegiate Church of St Peter, to give it its correct title, have been crowned the kings and queens of England from William the Conqueror to Elizabeth II. The Coronation chair made for Edward I is set above the Stone of Scone, itself a coronation seat for Scottish kings until brought here as a symbol of Scotland's subjection. During the actual ceremony the chair is covered with cloth of gold and moved into the sanctuary before the high altar.

A church supposedly existed here in Saxon times, but the first verifiable records date from the foundation of a Benedictine abbey dedicated to St Peter in 750, known as the West Monastery or Westminster because of its relationship to the City of London. It was rebuilt on a worthier scale by Edward the Confessor but did not really begin to assume its present shape until Henry III conceived something grander in honour of the canonised St Edward, whose remains had been laid behind the altar. Sir Christopher Wren renewed some of the stonework and planned a central tower which never materialised; but one of his pupils was responsible for the west towers.

From Henry III's time onwards the abbey became a burial place for most rulers until George II, many preserved in wax effigy in the museum, and also for some of the country's most distinguished commoners: David Livingstone and the Unknown Warrior of the First World War lie here, and there are writers such as Blake, Browning, Tennyson, Dickens and Hardy. One American, George Peabody, was buried in the abbey in 1869, but his remains were later removed to Massachusetts.

Parliament Square, London

This spacious plaza at the end of Whitehall allows one to stand back and contemplate Westminster Abbey, St. Margaret's – parish church of the House of Commons since the early seventeenth century – and the Houses of Parliament themselves without danger of being run over, which is more than can be said of many of London's vantage points.

Edward the Confessor lived in Westminster Palace, which ceased to be a royal residence after a fire in 1512. The renovated buildings were occupied by the Lords and Commons until another, finally destructive fire in 1834. Sir Charles Barry laid out the square as an integral part of his concept for the new Houses of Parliament in 1840.

During the second World War various buildings suffered repeated damage from air raids, and in May 1941 the House of Commons was gutted, to be restored immediately after the war by Sir Giles Gilbert Scott.

The 320-ft clock tower of the New Palace of Westminster is usually miscalled Big Ben, which is in fact the name of the 13½-ton bell on which the hours strike. The 'Ben' was Sir Benjamin Hall, Commissioner of Works at the time of the bell's installation. A light at the top of the tower after dark indicates that the House is still sitting.

The bearded visionary in the foreground is Epstein's statue of Field-Marshal Smuts. Most of the other statues in the square are of Prime Ministers, but there is also one of Abraham Lincoln, presented by the people of the United States.

The Houses of Parliament, London

William Wordsworth, spellbound on Westminster Bridge at dawn, was of the opinion that

Earth has not anything to show more fair;
Dull would he be of soul who could pass by
A sight so touching in its majesty:
This city now doth, like a garment, wear
The beauty of the morning; silent, bare,
Ships, towers, domes, theatres, and temples lie
Open unto the fields, and to the sky:
All bright and glittering in the smokeless air.

The fields are far to find, the sky is more than somewhat hazed, the silence stands little chance against traffic on the bridge and the whine of jet aircraft descending towards Heathrow, and even the sternest abatement measures have not yet produced what could reasonably be called smokeless air; there are contemporary eyesores on all sides, throwing the few remaining joys of old London hopelessly out of proportion; yet even among the tower blocks and the internal combustion engines there can, on a misty nostalgic evening, remain a faint tang of that Never-Never-London which has inspired so many painters and poets and novelists.

Against the sky, defying the glassy shimmer of the modern temple on Millbank in the background, the Victoria Tower remains darkly confident. Through its entrance the Sovereign arrives for the State opening of Parliament; and the public comes to study the behaviour of its elected representatives and the statues and mementoes of their predecessors.

Trafalgar Square, London

The square itself was laid out in 1829 by Sir Charles Barry to commemorate Lord Nelson's triumph from his appropriately named flagship, *Victory*, over the French navy in a battle which resulted in his death but also in the death of Napoleon's hopes of ruling the seas. It was not until 1840 that a committee assembled to consider the most fitting public tribute to the great admiral himself, of whom the Polish immigrant Joseph Conrad was later to write:

> *Other men there were, ready and able to add to the treasure of victories the British navy has given to the nation. It was the lot of Lord Nelson to exalt all this glory . . . through the fidelity of his fortune and the power of his inspiration, he stands unique among the leaders of fleets and sailors. He brought heroism into the line of duty.*

Some critics objected to any column which might block the view of the National Gallery. Another thought it ought to be kept to one side of the square, in case some worthier figure than Nelson might eventually need a mightier memorial. At last it was agreed that a column bearing the now familiar figure should be raised to more than 200-ft above the ground – a height soon reduced because of trepidation about the column's behaviour in high winds. Work was completed in 1849 save for Landseer's bronze lions, which were added almost 20 years later.

St Paul's Cathedral, London

In 1666 the Great Fire of London began in a Pudding Lane bakery and spread so rapidly and devastatingly that John Evelyn, stunned, could only record in his diary:

> *The conflagration was so universal, and the people so astonished, that . . . they hardly stirred to quench it; so that there was nothing heard, or seen, but crying out and lamentation, running about like distracted creatures, without at all attempting to save even their goods, such a strange consternation there was upon them.*

Among the buildings destroyed was the medieval St Paul's Cathedral, but within a week of the fire's dying down Christopher Wren had submitted plans for a revivified city, of which the new cathedral was to be the cornerstone.

Another fire raged around it in December 1940, and during this and other air raids much of the stained glass was shattered; but the cathedral survived, and the introduction of clear glass, as originally specified by Wren, has brought new light to the vast interior.

The crypt holds Nelson's massive tomb and Wellington's 18-ton funeral carriage, in which the Iron Duke's body was drawn to St Paul's in 1852 by 12 black horses. But the man worthiest to rest in the cathedral is surely Sir Christopher Wren himself, his epitaph (translated) justly declaring

> *if you seek his monument, look around.*

(Overleaf) Salisbury Cathedral, Wiltshire

The original Old Sarum, two miles north of the present Salisbury, was inhabited almost without interruption from the Iron Age onwards. Early in the thirteenth century Bishop Herbert Poore, weary of wrangles with local worthies and with the problems of an inadequate water supply, and downcast by the destruction of his cathedral in a cataclysmic thunderstorm, petitioned Richard I to be allowed to move his community to a happier location. Granted a site at New Sarum on the river Avon, he did not live to see work commence; but in 1220 his brother laid the foundation stone of this proud Gothic edifice, and in 1258 it was consecrated in the presence of Henry III and Queen Eleanor. The incomparable cloisters were begun five years later.

The spire was not added until the fourteenth century, and if it had been allowed for in the original plans the foundations would probably have been strengthened to carry this extra weight. Over and over again during succeeding decades it has been found necessary to bolster up the tower and check the sagging inclination of the spire, at 404-ft the loftiest in England. Among those called in to the rescue at one stage was Sir Christopher Wren, whose report can be studied in the cathedral library.

Salisbury is Trollope's Barchester, Hardy's Melchester. The hospitality of its Archdeacon Fisher and his uncle, the Bishop, encouraged Constable to paint his masterpieces of the cathedral and water meadows.

Willy Lott's Cottage, Flatford, Suffolk

Early in the eighteenth century the Constable family crossed the river Stour from Essex and settled in Suffolk, to become prosperous mill-owners. Born at East Bergholt in 1776, John Constable was expected to follow the family tradition, but from early youth was obsessed by the desire to become a painter. He was to travel far, but was always drawn back to the slow river in its shimmering vale.

> *Painting with me is another word for feeling, and I associate my careless boyhood with all that lies on the banks of the Stour; those scenes made me a painter.*

The scenes have not altered too irrevocably since his day. Flatford Mill, though pressed too closely by cafés and souvenir sellers and by coachloads of visitors on sunny days, is still there. Willy Lott's cottage, painted from different angles as a separate subject or as part of other compositions such as *The Hay Wain*, stands where it always stood.

Willy Lott lived here for 80 years and claimed never to have been away or wished to be away from home for more than four days together. He lived to see his young friend John gain recognition after painful struggles, but was probably bemused by the interest shown by faraway people in representations of his simple cottage.

Willy is buried, and his gravestone may be seen, in East Bergholt churchyard.

Market Place, Lavenham, Suffolk

The timbered houses are largely the result of an influx of Flemish weavers in the late fourteenth century. The prosperity of many a Suffolk town was based on the wool trade, and Lavenham's mighty church owes its existence as much to Thomas Spring 'the Rich Clothier' as to the thirteenth Earl of Oxford, who conceived it as a thank-offering on his safe return from the Wars of the Roses, in which he led the vanguard of Henry VII's army at the battle of Bosworth.

In the Market Place the clothiers established their superb Guildhall, preserved in fine condition today in spite of its sad degradation to the status of prison during the wool industry's decline – a prison kept in such poor repair that inmates were known to kick their way out through the plaster walls. It is now administered by the National Trust.

Many houses in the Market Place date from the same era, though others are later intruders: temporary stalls set up for fairs and markets slyly established themselves in more substantial form. In 1938 it was found necessary to condemn and demolish cottages which were obscuring the Guildhall itself.

The market cross is in fact an ecclesiastical wayside cross, from which at some stage the cross-piece was removed and the existing ball substituted at the top.

King's College Chapel, Cambridge

The foundations of Cambridge University were laid, spiritually if not materially, by early thirteenth-century students who came to this edge of the bleak fenland region to gather round often controversial religious and lay teachers whose ideas appealed to them. The first college to be formally established was Peterhouse, in 1280.

In 1441 Henry VI founded King's, planning that a number of 'king's scholars' from the preparatory school he had set up the previous year in Eton should, after sufficient grounding in grammar, be sent to this new college. The Chapel was begun in 1446 with white magnesian limestone arduously transported from Yorkshire. The cost of construction was to be defrayed largely from the revenues of the Duchy of Lancaster and from the seizure of the assets of foreign religious foundations. Interrupted by the Wars of the Roses, it took almost a century to complete. With the incomparable fan vaulting of its soaring stone roof it is perhaps the finest example of Perpendicular architecture we have.

Every Christmas Eve is held the now famous Festival of Nine Lessons and Carols.

The loveliest prospect of most of the colleges is from the Backs, the lawns and gardens fringing the river Cam, here crossed by an attractive sequence of bridges. King's bridge dates only from 1818 when it replaced an earlier one some distance to the north.

Elm Hill, Norwich, Norfolk

Norwich is both a modern and a medieval city. Its far-sighted planners have contained many smart shopping areas within traffic-free streets and precincts; but its old ghosts must still feel at home in many a wayward alley and secluded courtyard, in the well-maintained old buildings, and in the spacious cathedral close. There are chain stores and busy factories; there are also distinguished merchants' houses of past centuries and over 30 medieval churches.

Originally the city had two distinct focal points: the Saxon market place on Tombland (a sinister word deriving innocently from the Saxon 'toom', meaning a patch of open land), and the Norman market place still on the slope below the 1938 City Hall. Near one side of Tombland is cobbled Elm Hill, perhaps too prettily given over to rather precious little shops – but better this than abject surrender to the plate-glass, deep-freeze world.

On its crest, one old church has been turned into a museum of ecclesiastical art. At its foot, another rescued from neglect has become a Boy Scout headquarters.

In 1861 a monastery was founded on the hill by the self-styled Father Ignatius, who wished to revive monasticism within the Church of England and whose disciples credited him with miraculous powers. There were acrimonious arguments in the district, and finally the brotherhood fled to Wales.

ELM HILL CRAFT SHOP
ELM HILL CRAFT SHOP
R. TOWNSHEND
ANTIQUES
THE STAMP CORNER

Thurne Mill, Norfolk Broads

The river Yare provides a meandering thoroughfare from Norwich to Great Yarmouth, and so to the Broads. It was long believed that these open stretches of water were the legacy of some freakish glacial action, but more recently it has been established that most of the lakes resulted from man-made peat or turf diggings. Linked by a web of streams, rivers, fleets and dykes, the breezy expanses carry in summer a volume of traffic which threatens to outdo the wheeled traffic of our crowded cities; but those who fall in love with the region usually find their own special back-water, and with experience will choose the right time of year, the right point of departure, and the right route to follow.

Over 4,000 acres of the area are maintained by the Norfolk Naturalists' Trust as nature reserves, offering safety for the breeding of many of our own rarer birds, and hospitality to a growing number of migratory visitors.

Windmills, especially pumping mills, used to be a feature of the Broads, but Thurne mill and those at Hornsey and Berney Arms are among the few still preserved in reasonable condition.

Not far from Thurne Mouth are the misshapen remains of St Benet's Abbey, founded in the ninth century, abandoned in Henry VIII's time – when villagers helped themselves to its stones to build their houses – and suffering its final indignity 200 years ago when its arched gatehouse was distorted by the base of a huge windmill, itself now a humped, incongruous part of the ruin.

A849

'Boston Stump', Lincolnshire

St Botolph gave his name to Botolph's Town, now Boston, with the foundation of a monastery in 654, later sacked by the Danes. The 272-ft tower of the church dedicated to him provides a landmark and seamark known as the Boston Stump, dominating miles of the flat Lincolnshire countryside and clearly visible from the far side of the Wash. The church was largely built during the reign of Edward III, its interior having a high embossed roof and some finely carved choir stalls.

In the early seventeenth century some of the Pilgrim Fathers were imprisoned in the Guildhall. Later they acquired many local recruits, some of whom set sail in the *Mayflower* in 1620. There were so many Boston men on the seven ships which set off under the Rev. Isaac Johnson in 1630 that the capital of Massachusetts was called after their home town. In memory of this the American city has given generous contributions towards the restoration of St Botolph's church.

In the time of King John, Boston's maritime trade almost rivalled that of London. The silting up of the river Witham reduced the town to somnolence for some centuries, but at the end of the last century the river was deepened and extensive work carried out on the docks. A new quay was opened just before the Second World War.

BATEMAN'S
GOOD HONEST
ALES

Petergate, York

Eboracum was the military capital of Roman Britain, and in A.D. 306 Constantine was proclaimed Emperor here. By the late fourth century there was already a Bishop of York, and by the seventh century the post had been elevated to an archbishopric, still second only to that of Canterbury.

The walls of York tell the story of successive powers. The Romans originally protected their settlement with a high earth rampart, to which Severus added a stone wall with a tower at each corner: one, the Multangular tower, survives. William the Conqueror set up earth and timber walls. Today we can walk for two or three miles along white walls from the Middle Ages, with a few breaks here and there and with the openings of four gates or bars giving access to the heart of the city.

Petergate enters through the western gate, Bootham Bar, which retains its portcullis. Along it there is an alluring view of the towers of the Cathedral of St Peter, usually known as York Minster. Begun in 1154 on the site of a wooden church in which the pagan king Edwin consented to be baptised, it took over 300 years to build. Its rich stained glass was saved from destruction through the Civil War and through both World Wars. The Minster itself narrowly escaped destruction in 1829, when a madman named Jonathan Martin set it on fire.

In our own day there are fresh dangers: the vibration of heavy traffic threatens to shake foundations and fabric apart.

FARMERS
BUTCHERS
SCOTT
THE PORK BUTCHER
ARMERS BUTCHERS
ORK HAMS BACON LARD
ANTIQUES

(Overleaf) Robin Hood's Bay, Yorkshire

From the 600-ft cliff of Ravenscar northward the North Sea scoops out an arc ending at the headland of North Cheek. Huddled in a gulley cut through the cliffs where they sag to no more than 100-ft above sea level is a little town whose name has no official sanction. The correct name of the parish, with its scattering of neighbouring hamlets, is Fylingdales; but this part of it has been called Robin Hood's Bay for so long that it is unlikely to change now.

The most frequently quoted explanatory legend is that Robin of Barnesdale (or of Locksley, or Huntingdon, whichever source one favours) often visited the region because of the temptations in rich Whitby and its abbey, and that when he and his merry men were being hotly pursued by enemies they fled to the bay and escaped in boats which were kept always ready for them. Another local tradition is that the mounds called Robin Hood Butts on the moor behind were the scene of longbow practice by the outlaws; but unromantic experts have shown these to be prehistoric barrows.

Strengthening the case of Robin's having been a local lad is a reference in a thirteenth-century Yorkshire pipe roll to 'Robertus Hood fugitivus'.

More massive than the mounds on the moor are the modern, even futuristic, three white globes of Fylingdales Early Warning Station on their three black thrones.

Bolton Abbey and the River Wharfe, Yorkshire

The Yorkshire Dales, scoured out of the Pennine range by tributaries of the river Ouse, stretch southwards from the Durham border almost to Leeds. The Pennine Way footpath crosses part of the Dales on its 250-mile progress up 'the backbone of England'.

Of them all, the loveliest is perhaps Wharfedale, through which the river Wharfe, rising near lonely Pen-y-ghent, descends on its 60-mile journey to join the Ouse. A few miles north of Bolton Abbey it rages through a gorge known as the Strid, from an Old English word meaning turmoil; but it is clear and tranquil as it winds through the meadows past these skeletal ruins.

The shell is that of a priory founded in 1151. The nave, last restored in 1864, is used now as the parish church.

Monasteries in this region possessed extensive rights over grazing land, and were always trying to extend their sheep-farming activities. There were many boundary disputes as bitter as those of the ranches of the American Wild West, resulting in the marking out – sometimes by common consent, sometimes after protracted squabbles between monks and peasants – of boundaries by drystone walls, long stretches of which perform a useful function to this day.

Housesteads, Northumberland

Once called the Picts' Wall in reluctant tribute to the invaders it was meant to keep at bay, the 90-mile Roman fortification from Wallsend-on-Tyne to Bowness-on-Solway is now usually referred to by the name of the Emperor Hadrian who visited Britain in A.D. 122 and ordered his governor here to erect a barrier 10-ft thick right across the country. There was to be a castle every mile, with two turrets as watchtowers between each castle.

At wider intervals larger forts were constructed to hold sizeable garrisons, complete with bath-houses for the soldiers and storage space for food and weapons. Housesteads is one of the best preserved of these. The outlines of barracks, stables and granaries have been uncovered, and not far away is an equally impressive milecastle with an imposing gateway. A museum opened here by the National Trust contains maps, models, and some of the pottery and coins found during excavations along the wall.

Hadrian's successor began work on fortifications even further north, between the Forth and the Clyde, and neglected the older barrier. This new Antonine Wall was overrun several times by Picts and Scots, and in due course it proved necessary to fall back on Hadrian's Wall and strengthen it. It was in use until the end of the fourth century when, after three penetrations by Picts and Scots, eventually joined by Saxons, its forts were expanded into fortified villages and then finally abandoned.

Wooler and the Cheviot Hills, Northumberland

For much of their length the Cheviot Hills form the border between England and Scotland, their highest point being The Cheviot, 2,676-ft above Wooler. The region is famous for its black-faced and Cheviot sheep. Between the range and Hadrian's Wall to the south lies a large part of the Northumberland National Park, and the Pennine Way from the Derbyshire Peak District reaches its end against these slopes. This is splendid walking country, and the river Till is a fisherman's paradise.

South of Wooler market place are remains of a Norman castle, typical of many gaunt ruins in local villages, once guardians of the military and trade routes running from south to north.

Near Wooler was born Josephine Grey, the nineteenth-century social reformer who as Josephine Butler fought beside the feminist crusaders of The Ladies National Association For The Abolition Of Government Regulations Of Vice. On the house in Wooler where she died is a plaque presented by the local Women's Institute.

Derwentwater and Skiddaw, Cumberland

The oldest rocks in the Lake District are the Skiddaw Slates, formed from the erosion by rain and rivers of the remains of still older rocks from the turbulent sea-bed of 500 million years ago. Volcanic eruptions and Ice Age glaciers caused the folding and buckling of the surface in which the lakes formed. They are all now diminishing in size because of a steady process of silting up.

The largest stretch of water, once reaching from the head of Derwentwater to Bassenthwaite, has now been cut in two, and some smaller tarns have already disappeared altogether.

Derwentwater is three miles long and about a mile wide, and reflects one of the most colourful mixtures in Lakeland – bleak crags, glowing fells and the changing hues of woodland plunging steeply down to its banks. A footpath keeps close to the shore for a considerable distance. Energetic walkers can attain the peak of 3,054-ft Skiddaw without too much peril if they choose the right approach – a route up which eighteenth-century travellers preferred to use sturdy ponies.

It was in that century that Dr John Brown, one of the earliest tourists in the region, declared in a study of Keswick that Derwentwater had, above all others, the true qualities of picturesque landscape:

Beauty, horror, and immensity.

Langdale, Westmorland

The glacial valley of Langdale, with its old paths, packhorse bridges and stepping stones, is overlooked by the twin crags of the Langdale Pikes. A little way to the east is Grasmere, where William Wordsworth settled in 1799, receiving in 1813 the sinecure of distributor of stamps for Westmorland. He made Lakeland his own as surely as Constable made the Stour valley his own, and in his guide to the region urged the visitor to conjure up a vision of the processes of its creation and its special qualities:

> *He may see or hear in fancy the winds sweeping over the lakes, or piping with a loud voice among the mountain peaks and, lastly, may think of the primeval woods shedding and renewing their leaves with no human eye to notice, or human heart to regret or welcome the change.*

Today the reality all too often cancels out the dream vision. A fast modern motorway through the heart of the Lake District is under discussion. Even without it, the existing roads carry visitors all too ready to speed on without concern for what they leave behind: four men work full-time throughout the holiday season collecting tons of litter; six park wardens and 300 volunteers have to devote much of their time to the same task; and an average of 25 abandoned motor cars a year have to be removed from the lakesides.

Little Moreton Hall, Cheshire

With Elizabeth I firmly settled on the throne and her enemies kept resolutely at bay, the country's self-assurance began to show itself in its domestic architecture. Castles and fortified manors were no longer necessary. Some were converted into more comfortable residences; and many new, smaller manor houses were built by the lesser gentry and prospering merchants.

Stone and brick were shaped into pleasing patterns rather than into dour defences. Imaginatively combined timber and plaster made the most of the country's natural resources. Before Elizabeth's time most reliable glass had been imported, but now French workmen came to settle in England and set new standards for the industry here.

Old Moreton Hall, or Little Moreton Hall, is an outstanding example of a black-and-white timbered, moated manor house. It was built by the Moreton family between 1559 and 1589 on the site of an earlier, probably fortified, mansion. Outside there are great flourishes of carved gables, corner-posts and doors. Within, heraldic carvings embellish the fireplaces, and the long gallery retains its original panelling.

Around the turn of the century the hall was split into apartments for working-class tenants, but has now come into the hands of the National Trust.

Dovedale, Derbyshire

At Edale near the flattened crown of Kinder Peak, *the* Peak of England's first National Park in the Derbyshire Peak District, the Pennine Way begins its long pilgrimage towards the northern palisade of the Cheviots. The gritty severity of the High Peak mellows in the south into a limestone land through which the river Dove, on its way from the hills to join the river Trent, cuts a gorge which John Ruskin lauded as

an alluring lesson in all that is admirable.

Famous as a trout stream, the Dove was fished by Izaak Walton, and *The Compleat Angler*, actually completed by his friend Charles Cotton, tells of conversations and discoveries as the two of them worked their way along its banks. 'Good God', said Cotton, 'how sweet are all things here.' It is said that a stroll beside the stream inspired Handel to begin the composition of *Messiah*. Dovedale was the Happy Valley of Johnson's *Rasselas*, the Eagle Dale of George Eliot's *Adam Bede*.

There was an incredible attempt by the War Office in 1947 to extend its firing ranges so that access to the 20 stepping stones which cross the river and thereby cross the border between Derbyshire and Staffordshire should be barred to the public. The authorities seemed surprised that this should give rise to stormy protests; but they speedily acknowledged defeat.

PLEASE KEEP THIS
ENTRANCE CLEAR

Lord Leycester's Hospital, Warwick

The county town of Warwickshire, with its fourteenth-century castle mirrored in the river Avon, is noted for one earl whose machinations were primarily responsible for the execution of Joan of Arc, and another whose machinations led him to be dubbed 'the King-maker'. It also, however, profited from benevolent lords such as Robert Dudley, Earl of Leicester, who in 1571 took over the buildings of the combined Guilds of Holy Trinity and St George to provide the basis of a hospital by the west gate. Later two adjoining timber-framed houses were incorporated.

The chapel straddles the fourteenth-century gateway. The chaplain resides in the east wing of the hospital, the master in the north wing.

In the banqueting hall Fulke Greville entertained James I, who created him first Baron Brooke and granted him Warwick Castle. On his tombstone in St Mary's church he left the boast:

Servant to Queen Elizabeth,
Counceller to King James,
Frend to Sir Philip Sidney,
Trophaeum Peccati.

Like his admired Philip Sidney, he was a generous and cultured human being, so it was all the more tragic that he should have met his death at the hands of a servant who, resentfully suspecting that no provision had been made for him in his master's will, stabbed him and then killed himself.

THE
LORD LEYCESTER
HOSPITAL
Teas - Coffee
Light Refreshments

Compton Wynyates, Warwickshire

Early in the fifteenth century the then Duke of Bedford destroyed the church and village of Fulbrook, near Warwick, in order to lay out a park. A hundred years later the bricks from his castle, itself by then derelict, were taken by Sir William Compton for use in the construction of a house near the abandoned village of Compton Superior. The 'Wynyates' added to the family name is interpreted by some as Old English for 'the vale through which the wind blows', by others as a corruption of 'vineyard': either is more appealing than the earlier name of Compton-in-the-Hole.

Built around an inner courtyard, the manor is a glowing example of Tudor craftsmanship, with corkscrew chimneys, the arms of Henry VIII and Catherine of Aragon on the porch, and a much later surround of extravagant topiary.

In 1618 Lord Compton was created Earl of Northampton. The second baron is hero of a romantic story telling of his love for a London merchant's heiress whom he smuggled out of her Canonbury home in a bread-basket.

During the Civil War, Roundheads used the house and chapel as a barracks, smashed much of the stained glass, threw the Compton monuments in the moat and filled it in, and destroyed the nearby church, which was rebuilt in 1665. Greater disaster threatened when the eighth earl, after squandering his money on an abortive election in Northampton, ordered the whole place to be pulled down. Fortunately his steward loved it too much to obey and did no more than brick up the windows to save window tax, until such time as the family fortunes improved.

Stratford-upon-Avon, Warwickshire

Originally established by the Guild of the Holy Cross, Stratford's Grammar School is one of the oldest of its kind in England. The Guild had built a chapel in 1269, and in 1417 added the school for the education of its members' sons. Following the suppression of the Guild the buildings were granted by the Crown to the Corporation of the town, but in 1553 Edward VI refounded the school, and today the chapel functions as the school chapel. It has a disconcertingly vivid 'Doom' and other medieval wall paintings.

It seems reasonably certain that William Shakespeare would have received his early education here, even if he did come to it creeping like snail, unwillingly, and acquire from it small Latin and less Greek.

There is also a strong probability that Shakespeare's first encounter with the drama was in the Guild Hall. His father, a prosperous burgess, is known to have been bailiff during visits by troupes of strolling players, and as such it was his prerogative to invite leading townsfolk to performances in the hall: William would surely have been allowed to join the audience.

Coventry Cathedral, Warwickshire

In 1043 Lady Godiva and Earl Leofric began work on an abbey church which was later ravaged by Henry VIII, rebuilt, and raised to cathedral status in 1918. In November 1940 worse destruction was poured upon it from Nazi bombers.

In June 1950 an architectural competition for the construction of a new cathedral was opened, prefaced by the injunction:

> *The Cathedral is to speak to us and to generations to come of the Majesty, the Eternity and the Glory of God. God, therefore, direct you.*

When the news reached Basil Spence that his report and drawings had been chosen, he went to sit in St Paul's Cathedral, overcome, he confesses, by *the awful feeling that the finger had pointed at me, and that I was not worthy or able.* Time has happily proved him wrong.

Spence called on his most gifted contemporaries for contributions to match his basic concept. Graham Sutherland's great tapestry of Christ in glory came into being; Epstein's St Michael soars above the Devil on the wall beside the baptistry window. John Piper designed the stained glass of the window itself as an abstract composition which would not clash with Sutherland's tapestry. The deeply modelled stone, 81-ft high by 51-ft across, contains 198 lights, the centre producing a radiant sunburst. The boulder for the font below it was brought from the Holy Land.

Worcester Cathedral and the River Severn

Worcester was appointed as the site of a new see late in the seventh century, and by the Middle Ages had become a flourishing city, with the cathedral pretty much in its present form. In the centre of the Early English choir stands the tomb of King John, who asked in his will that he should be buried in the city of which he was so fond.

The first bridge across the Severn was wooden, but the monks built a stone one in 1313 which lasted for more than 450 years. On the west bank below the present bridge is the most fortunately, beautifully situated of all county cricket grounds.

In 1651 Charles II and the remnants of his weary Scottish troops sought refuge here, but after Cromwell had attacked and routed them, the young King rode off and, so legend has it, hid in an oak tree until it was possible for him to be spirited away and finally smuggled out of the country.

Much of the Georgian elegance of the city itself has been ruined by uncoordinated modern building, just as in the cathedral there has been some discordant Victorian restoration. But there is still much harmony here. The annual Three Choirs Festival, inaugurated in 1724 *for the benefit of widows and orphans in those dioceses*, is shared between Worcester, Gloucester and Hereford. Their three cathedral choirs form the nucleus of vocal forces singing in each city in rotation, and each year the programme, devoted mainly to oratorios and other choral works but with orchestral music also, is under the jurisdiction of the host cathedral's organist.

Symond's Yat, Herefordshire

The word 'yat' means, in the nearby Forest of Dean, a gate or a pass. 'Symond's' is associated by some with a remote Sigemund, by others with Robert Symonds, a former High Sheriff of Herefordshire who owned extensive property in the neighbourhood during the seventeenth century.

About four miles into the county from the Monmouthshire border, the rock itself is just over 500-ft above sea level, and from its top commands views which take in Ross-on-Wye, the dizzying uprush of the Coldwell Rocks, and the Welsh mountains.

It is on the slopes of one of those mountains, Plynlimmon, that the river Wye rises, making its winding course through this luxuriant region of cider apple orchards to the Bristol Channel. Famous for salmon and trout, it describes a five-mile loop here around Huntsham Hill, across which are three parallel ditches and ramparts of a Roman camp – one of many such in the region.

Tewkesbury Abbey, Gloucestershire

Close to the confluence of the rivers Severn and Avon, the abbey is thought to stand on the site of a seventh-century church built by Theoc, from whom the town takes its name: in Domesday Book it was spelt Teodekesberie.

The mighty tower, 132-ft high and 46-ft square, is a flawless example of Norman architecture; the Norman arch of the west front holds a great window installed in 1686; the porch is Norman; and within there are Norman columns in the nave and Norman walls to the aisles.

When the building was threatened by Henry VIII's iconoclasts, it was saved by the indignant townspeople, who had always shared it on terms of mutual affection with the monks and regarded it as part of their own heritage.

A famous battle was fought here in 1471. The Duke of York, seizing on the madness of Henry VI as an excuse to proclaim himself King Edward IV, rushed to Tewkesbury to intercept the forces of Henry's warlike queen, Margaret. The Prince of Wales fell in the battle, and Margaret's troops were defeated. Some sought sanctuary in the abbey but were dragged out for execution in the market place.

The Duke of Clarence who is reputed to have met his death by drowning in a butt of Malmsey is buried behind the high altar and commemorated in a brass. There is also a medallion portrait of Mrs Craik, who wrote of the town as Nortonbury in her novel, *John Halifax, Gentleman*.

Chipping Campden, Gloucestershire

The stone which gives the Cotswolds their characteristic mellow appearance is a limestone whose softness is responsible for the gently rounded, undulating contours of the hills. The fine-grained freestone is easily cut into blocks immediately after it has been quarried, but hardens on exposure. The porosity of the roof tiles, taken from surface quarries, makes it advisable to pitch the roofs very steeply so that rain and snow will not linger on them.

This is not thickly wooded country, and on the bleaker slopes of the wolds the material for stiles and gateposts, and for the fencing of fields and orchards, has inevitably had to be the local stone, close to the surface and there for the taking.

The town quarry near Horseman's Corner above Westington provided most of the stone used in building Chipping Campden, showing at its best in the seventeenth-century almshouses which so congenially offset the fifteenth-century church. This owes much of its richness to the prosperous days of the wool trade. Four admirably preserved portrait brasses in the floor of the chancel all commemorate wool merchants.

In the eighteenth century an avenue of limes dedicated to the Twelve Apostles was planted as an approach to the church.

Cirencester, Gloucestershire

The Roman settlement of *Corinium Dubonnorum* grew up at a crossing of the Churn, one of the two headstreams of the river Thames. It was first a small military station, then an important road junction: the Fosse Way, Ermine Street and Akeman Street all meet here. Just outside modern Cirencester are the Querns, earthworks and remains of a Roman amphitheatre.

The 134-ft Perpendicular tower of the parish church and its huge sixteenth-century porch rise straight from the Market Place. Much of the cost of the porch was met by local guilds, who used it as a guildhall. It also served as Town Hall and even as a burial-place. In 1836 the ornately carved stonework was repaired, but weathered badly and was in danger of crumbling away. The whole façade was then taken down and reassembled stone by stone.

The church possesses fine medieval glass in its east and west windows, and many richly carved screens in both stone and wood. A statue of John the Baptist on the tower has a face so blackened by time that the street on which it looks down has been nicknamed, and will always be known as, Black Jack Street.

HUNT TAILORS
HORTON CHEMIST
OXFORD ADAMSONS LTD

The Botanic Garden and Magdalen Tower, Oxford

The Botanic Garden, behind high walls opposite Magdalen College, is the oldest in Great Britain. It was once a Jewish cemetery, and beside the entrance is a Hebrew cryptogram on the year 1290, when the Jews were driven out of the country.

Magdalen College was founded beside the river Cherwell in 1448, work on its beautiful tower beginning in 1492. At sunrise on the first day of May the college choir sings the May Morning hymn from the top.

James II tried in 1687 to force a Papist nominee into the Presidency. This was against the college statutes, and the Fellows defiantly elected their own candidate. The Court of Ecclesiastical Commission, under the infamous Judge Jeffreys, took them to task; but they all chose expulsion rather than compliance. A public fund was opened on their behalf. At last King James gave in and allowed them to return and instal their own nominee. Ever since then, 25th October has been celebrated as Restoration Day with a peal of the tower's ten bells and the toast, *Justice for All.* To this day Magdalen is remembered for its *tower James II ran his head against.*

In the last century there was a plan to build a railway station right beside Magdalen Bridge, abandoned when the railway company found it was, one might say, running its engine against a wall just as unyielding as that of Jacobean times.

Blenheim Palace, Oxfordshire

After inflicting a decisive defeat on the French and their allies at Blenheim in 1704, John Churchill, first Duke of Marlborough, came home to England in triumph. He was granted the royal manor of Woodstock, once a game preserve for Anglo-Saxon kings, and promised a sumptuous palace whose glories should keep the glories of his victory evergreen in the minds of his grateful countrymen.

Unfortunately the gratitude and the funds diminished as work progressed. Marlborough's political enemies lost no chance of attacking him; the Treasury made its payments with increasing reluctance; the Marlboroughs themselves had to pay for the final stages. Sarah, the Duchess, had been a favourite of Queen Anne's but fell from grace. In spite of all setbacks she had great tapestries woven for the palace, rejoiced in its vast library, harangued artists and workmen alike, and quarrelled tempestuously with the architect.

Sir John Vanbrugh collaborated with Nicholas Hawksmoor on the building itself, and with Henry Wise, the Queen's own gardener, on the layout of the grounds. Some 60 years later the gardens were reshaped by Capability Brown, who dammed a stream to create the lake, and laid out trees in groups to form a plan of the battle of Blenheim, each battalion being represented by an individual plantation.

Sir Winston Churchill, descendant and biographer of Marlborough, was born in the palace in 1874.

(Overleaf) Stourhead Gardens, Wiltshire

In Salisbury cathedral a fine marble memorial depicts Sir Richard Colt Hoare sitting in a chair and studying a page of one of his own histories of Wiltshire. His family contributed generously and creatively to that history. His grandfather, Henry Hoare, was a banker who had a Palladian house built for himself at Stourhead in 1722 and, between 1740 and 1750, laid out for his pleasure and the pleasure of generations to come the landscape gardens, now in the hands of the National Trust.

The design is classical but with a strong element of the developing 'picturesque' landscape style, taking in a hilltop Temple of the Sun, a grotto and, seen across the waters of the lake, a trim little Temple of Flora. Above the gardens is King Alfred's Tower, built in 1766 as a memorial to the scholar and warrior who turned the tide against the Danish invaders of England.

Later hands have added rhododendrons and azaleas to the beeches and conifers, producing in early summer an unforgettable fiery glow over the surface of the lake.

Stonehenge, Wiltshire

The great bluestone at the centre of this megalithic monument is known as the Altar Stone. Some 256-ft away is the Heel Stone, over which the sun rises on Midsummer Morning as harbinger of the longest day of the year. This has led many theorists to associate Stonehenge with primitive sun-worship rites, though not with the Druids, in spite of the vigil romantically organised by the modern Druid sect every 21st June.

There is no evidence for the identification of the so-called Slaughter Stone with any sacrificial ritual; and although there have been assertions that the monument incorporates significant astronomical alignments, the many remodellings of the stone patterns over untold centuries make it difficult to draw any firm deductions.

The original conformation must have included the outer bank and ditch, to which were added the Heel Stone and the Aubrey Holes, a ring of 56 pits filled in but rediscovered by the diarist John Aubrey. A double circle of bluestones was set up later. Their source has been established as the Prescelly Hills in Wales, and it was long believed that the great slabs had been taken from a revered mystic circle there and transported by some staggering prehistoric feat across the Bristol Channel, up the Avon, and 20 miles overland. In 1971, new findings about this part of England during the Ice Age showed it to be just as plausible that the bluestones should have been carried by the ice flow out of Wales and on to Salisbury Plain.

Gold Hill, Shaftesbury, Dorset

The lush farmlands of the Blackmoor Vale are overlooked by a steep chalk escarpment on a spur of which, 700-ft above the vale, stands Shaftesbury, once known as Shaston and referred to as such in Thomas Hardy's novels.

King Alfred expanded an existing settlement into a town in 880 with the endowment of a Benedictine nunnery, of which his daughter was first abbess. After the murder in 978 of 18-year-old King Edward by his step-mother Elfrida, at Corfe Castle, the corpse was brought here. Edward was succeeded by his step-brother Ethelred who, together with the murderess, gave the town many rich endowments. The dead king was canonised, and the shrine of Edward the Martyr attracted many pilgrims until the Reformation put an end to such devotions. King Canute died here in 1035. At one time the town had 11 churches, in addition to the great abbey church whose excavated foundations are still visible.

Gold Hill, steep and uneven, retains its cobbles and its distinctive cottages of local green sandstone. From the top one may, on an exceptionally clear day, see as far as Glastonbury. In bygone days it was enviously said that if the abbot of Glastonbury were to wed the abbess of Shaftesbury, any child of their marriage would be richer than the king of England.

Oare and Exmoor, Somerset

A thousand years ago the high moorland spreading from Somerset into north-east Devon, reaching its peak at Dunkery Beacon, was a royal forest. In 1954 some 265 square miles were classified as a National Park. On this expanse of whispering bracken, grass and heather, grazed over by sheep, shaggy Exmoor ponies and red deer, the imagination also has every incitement to put forth its shoots.

Ever since R. D. Blackmore published *Lorna Doone* in 1869, scholars, enthusiasts and local historians have argued over the claims of rival combes to be the original of the valley in which the Doone clan of robbers and murderers lived, and from which Lorna was at last rescued by John Ridd, the strapping Exmoor yeoman.

The story, though one of the classics of romantic fiction, had a factual basis. Local records confirm the existence of a body of outlaws who did make their home in one of these remote valleys, terrorising their neighbours and unwary travellers.

Oare village has no doubts about the authenticity of its claims. Lorna's wedding is described by the author as taking place in its little church, and it was through a window on the south side of the chancel that Carver Doone shot her. In 1925 a medallion portrait was put up in the church to commemorate the centenary of Blackmore's birth.

Dunster, Somerset

A medieval village on the seaward rim of northern Exmoor, Dunster's importance as a harbour faded long ago because of the silting of the river mouth. It retains, however, one connection with the sea: at one end of its main street there remains an eighteenth-century tower built as a seamark.

From the other end of the street rears up the Norman castle, in a thousand years owned by only two families. In the Civil War it was attacked first by the King and then by Parliament, and during the later phases of the conflict was the only place in Somerset flying the royal standard. On a low mound behind the *Luttrell Arms*, the local inn named after the castellans of the last 600 years, are the remains of an embankment from which the Roundheads bombarded the defenders.

The yarn cross with its wide overhanging eaves and eight gabled windows, crowned by a lantern, has stood here since the early seventeenth century, sheltering the transactions of the yarn market. A short distance away is a pillar on broken steps, the ruin of another cross where butter was sold.

QUALITY
LEATHER
GOODS
CHEMIST

The Great Roman Bath, Bath, Somerset

The legendary King Bladud, father of King Lear, is traditionally associated with the establishment of the original Bath and the dedication of its medicinal waters, the only natural warm springs in England, to the goddess Minerva. In A.D. 44 the Romans set up their city of *Aquae Sulis* here with a temple, a forum, and fine houses. Their earliest baths were founded either by Vespasian or in the time of his son Titus. Some remains were uncovered 30-ft below ground in 1755 and then buried again. In 1883 further work was carried out and further extensive remains unearthed.

The lead flooring of the greatest of the Roman baths and segments of the lead conduits from spring to bath are still in position. The bath is encircled by a wide stone platform with six steps descending into the water, and there are remnants of seat recesses and the pillars which supported the roof. A stone culvert for carrying away waste water is as watertight as in the days of its installation.

An abbey is known to have existed in Saxon times. Its church was rebuilt between 1500 and 1600, and then much altered again by nineteenth-century restoration. On the front of its rectangular tower is a representation of Jacob's ladder.

(Overleaf) Lansdown Crescent, Bath, Somerset

At the beginning of the eighteenth century several things combined to raise Bath from the squalor into which it had sunk. Queen Anne paid a visit to take the waters, and it soon became fashionable to follow suit. Ralph Allen, a Cornishman who had made a fortune out of Bath stone and by carrying mails, settled in the town and financed the architect John Wood and his son to lay out their graceful squares, terraces and circuses. At the same time a Welsh-born gambler, Richard Nash, chose to come and try his fortunes here.

Beau Nash was pernickety in his dress and in his manner. He disapproved of the shoddiness of the ballrooms and gaming rooms, and laid down laws for their better operation. At his command a subscription list was established for keeping the Pump Room clean and providing an orchestra. In the heart of an attractive garden an Assembly Room was built, largely at his instigation. His code of dress and etiquette was not to be flouted. He imposed discipline on Bath society just as effectively as the Woods were imposing it on the shape of the town itself.

New gaming laws made things difficult for Nash, and by 1745 the end of his dandyish dictatorship was in sight. During the last penurious years of his life, Bath Corporation recognised the service he had done the community by making him a grant of £10 a month.

Lansdown Crescent, though in keeping with the Woods' ambience, was designed by John Palmer late in the century.

WICKS
WELLS

Tedburn St Mary, Devonshire

Kipling included cowslips from a Devon combe in his English posy. Hearty baritones assure us from pier pavilions and palm courts that there is nothing like Devonshire cream and cider, and yearn from bar to resonant bar for Devon, glorious Devon. Poets and novelists have long sung the praises of historic coastal towns such as Bideford and Plymouth, and of heroes such as Grenville, Hawkins, and above all Francis Drake, sailing to the west and returning with booty for himself and his rapacious Queen. The resort of Westward Ho! actually takes its name from the novel in which Charles Kingsley lauded the bravery of Devon men in the face of the Spanish Armada.

But between sea and sea exists the great inland expanse of Devon, our third largest county after Yorkshire and Lincolnshire. It encompasses the chill granite tors, bare slopes and prehistoric barrows of Dartmoor National Park as well as military firing ranges, moorland farms, and gentler pastures. There are hills and deep, convoluted lanes. Cottages seem to shoulder up from the earth rather than be set down upon it. A typical local style of building uses clay and straw mixed into what is known as cob, with a thatched roof above.

The swift-running streams enabled the county to wean the rich wool trade away from East Anglia after the invention of fulling machines operated by water instead of foot; but this, like the once extensive tin and copper mining, is almost forgotten now.

The River Dart at Totnes, Devonshire

The East and West Dart flow out of bleak Dartmoor to a junction at Dartmeet and on to the estuary of Dartmouth, becoming tidal below Totnes.

> *River Dart, O River Dart,*
> *Every year thou claim'st a heart.*

The roaring of the river at times of sudden flood has become known as 'the cry of the Dart', and a local superstition tells of this as an implacable demand for human sacrifice, not to be appeased until someone is drowned.

Totnes is one of the oldest boroughs in England, with winding streets, jagged-toothed remains of a Norman castle on a great mound, and two of its four original gates still in position. In the Middle Ages it grew rich on the cloth trade. It was chosen as one of the pumping stations along the line of Brunel's costly failure, the 'atmospheric' system of railway traction, in which air pressure through an iron pipe between the rails drove a piston connected to the engine. This was quiet, free from dust and fumes – and expensive. The system was abandoned within a year of its introduction.

Dartmouth, from which Richard Coeur de Lion set out on his crusades, was originally under the sway of the lords of Totnes, but clamoured for independence and won its own charter by the middle of the fourteenth century. It is now the home of the Royal Naval College.

Blackpool Sands, Start Bay, Devonshire

Between moor and sea, spreading south from Totnes, are the fertile South Hams, luxuriating in the mildest climate in the British Isles and offering roses in December. During the last war considerable stretches of the area and its coastal strip had to be relinquished to United States troops in training for the invasion and liberation of Europe, in recognition of which the U.S. authorities have set up an obelisk on the beach below Slapton.

The cliffs along Start Bay are mainly steep and grim, made of hard slate and grits, leading towards the even fiercer, wave-savaged coastline beyond Start Point. This ragged headland has a terrible reputation as a killer: in one night alone, a hideous March night in 1891, it claimed two ships and their crews.

At Blackpool Sands the rocks dip slightly to one of the gleaming beaches which break the harshness between Dartmouth and the headland. Local cattle are in the habit of sauntering down to join visitors in leisure hours on the shore.

Mevagissey, Cornwall

The Duchy of Cornwall was instituted in 1137 by Edward III for his elder son Edward, the Black Prince, and since that year the eldest son of the Sovereign has succeeded to the Dukedom by inheritance. The mild climate allows sub-tropical flowers and trees to grow here, and it is not surprising that the coast has been dubbed the Cornish Riviera, with its colourful fishing villages and sheltered harbours echoing those of the Mediterranean.

Mevagissey's name derives from two saints, Meva and Ida, whose church has some interesting monuments and a carved Norman font. Authentic records of the fishing community date back to 1410, but the settlement is probably even older. Like its neighbours and rivals, it subsisted for centuries almost entirely on the fruits of the sea - hake, cod, ling, and above all pilchards.

On adjoining cliff-tops the 'huer' would watch for traces of pilchard shoals on the water and then guide the seine boats from above by complex signalling. Catches were pressed and pickled in the fish 'cellars' which surrounded every courtyard, their conformations still easy to identify in many a courtyard house in the region.

At one time a season's catch could amount to 50,000 hogsheads of pilchards, but gradually the industry declined. Today's boats are used mainly for carrying visitors around the bays, or occasionally to take the more adventurous out shark-fishing.

Land's End, Cornwall

A drooping peninsula almost detached from the rest of England by the river Tamar, Cornwall is nowhere more than 15 miles or so from the sea or one of its inlets. 'Lessening by degrees like a horn', as one seventeenth-century writer described it, it ends in a stern promontory between 60 and 100-ft high – the westernmost tip of the English mainland. From this extremity to the farthest northerly point attainable on the mainland from here, John O'Groats on the Pentland Firth, is 873 miles.

Behind the cliffs and headlands are innumerable relics of prehistoric times. Iron Age forts dominate the hilltops. In the Land's End area alone there are over 20 of them. Later settlement was slow. It is not until after A.D. 900 that there is much trace of Anglo-Saxon names and influences creeping into the eastern end of the county. Celtic traditions and the Cornish form of the Celtic language lived on, and even today there is a stubborn patriotism in this ancient kingdom which has much in common with the stubborn granite of its coasts.

Over a mile out, the Longships Lighthouse stands among an outcrop of granite teeth, its light not merely a warning but also a welcome to many a thankfully returning voyager.

Others may use the ocean as their road,
Only the English make it their abode.

Even the most restless Englishman feels, sooner or later, how good it will be to come home.